How To Make Money In Stocks Value Investing Strategies

Book Wave Publications

Published by Book Wave Publications, 2023.

HOW TO MAKE MONEY IN STOCKS VALUE INVESTING STRATEGIES

First edition. August 27, 2023.

ISBN: 979-8223392743

Written by Book Wave Publications.

Also by Book Wave Publications

How To Make Money In Stocks Value Investing Strategies

Table of Contents

How To Make Money In Stocks Value Investing Strategies

Learn Investing Strategies For Beginners To Advanced Investors Investing In Stock Market

What You'll Learn

1. Learn the basics of moat based value investing employed by great investors
2. Get an investment framework to evaluate any stock idea
3. Learn how to identify if a business will be able to sustain its growth are not
4. Learn potential accounting red flags to watch-out for in any stock investment idea
5. Learn how to evaluate the management of the business you are looking to invest in.
6. Understand basics of financial statements including balance sheet, profit & loss statement & cash flow statement
7. Learn Common Size Analysis and Ratio Analysis to understand performance of any business

About The Book

This book will teach readers where and how to invest their money in respectable stocks. Most of the time, stock pickers follow advice without questioning the wisdom of investing in such programs. These Principles, which are based on a combination of Fundamentals, Valuations, and Technicals, are free to utilize right away. It can be learned in no more than two hours, and the advantages are long-lasting.

Grab the book!

Choosing stocks without researching their background, history, trend, industries, and governmental regulations could be risky. You must accept any losses, and you will gain from any gains. It is just your job to invest the money correctly because you worked hard to earn it.

The ability to make investments and earn income is one such skill. In order to make sound financial decisions on your own without seeking advice, you must have the necessary abilities. An excellent comparison to adopting advice without giving it any thought is gambling. Due to the high emotional stakes involved in gambling as well as the fact that you must pay brokerage fees and other taxes, the likelihood of losing is typically always greater than the likelihood of winning. Please keep in mind that whatever financial decision you make will have a direct influence on your family, especially your children.

I'll cover strategies—or rather filters—in this book that you can employ to create safer investments with respectable returns. I can guarantee you that if you choose stocks based on these factors, you won't ever need to depend on anyone and you'll be able to ignore any recommendations. You are accountable for your investment. Never skimp on knowledge when it comes to building your family and your fortune.I'll also talk about the free tools. If you are familiar with these strategies, you have 15 minutes to select any value stock.

Grab the book!

Who This Book Is For

1. People interested in learning how to invest in the stock market
2. People looking to generate consistent returns using value investing strategies
3. People looking for investment framework to analyze businesses
4. Perfect if you are more of a beginner and want all the foundational knowledge you can.
5. Great for stock market investors who want to go deeper into areas such as dividends, undervalued stocks, Spac, and more.
6. Excellent in terms of getting the full range of picking stocks from using value ratios to see if a current stock price is a good buy plus use of charts to make decisions.
7. Pick the Book you want to start in and finish the others when you have the time or as you progress in your investing journey.

Why Should I Invest In Stocks?

Please note that you shouldn't put all of your hard-earned money into stock investments. Invest money in equities that do not belong in your emergency fund or that you won't need for four to five years.

One approach to increase money is through stock investments. A person could have a variety of distinct financial objectives. One is a short-term objective with a one-year time frame.

A second is a medium-term objective, which can be set over a time frame of one to five years. The financial objectives listed below are long-term, or five-year or longer, in nature. Consider investing in debt funds with a fixed maturity if you have a short-term goal. Place a portion of your capital—60:40, or any other ratio—in debt funds and stocks.

The long-term objective is to invest (perhaps 25: 75) in gold and the stock market. Having term insurance, health insurance, and property insurance is generally a good idea. For medium- and long-term objectives, you should invest your money on the stock market. So let's examine the factors that influence stock purchases.

You have choices over where to put your money to work. The best approach to increase money, however, is through stock investing. You might remember that during the Pandemic (Corona), only necessities were permitted and there was never even a single day's worth of stock market closure.

Why does that matter?

It demonstrates how crucial the stock market is to our nation. It gauges the country's economic growth. Making a return of 22% should be simple if the stocks you choose follow the 11 Principles.

Let's look at a few real-world instances. Someone who invested $50,000 in a State Bank of India (SBI) fixed deposit 20 years ago would have gotten $45,000 instead of $50,000 due to the greater interest rate at the time.

As opposed to the company's FD, his acquaintance opted to invest in SBI shares. Then he received dividends, bonuses, splits, and share price benefits totaling Rs 122 lakhs. Each of the two is different from the other. In one instance, a person's investment increased from 4 lakhs to 122 lakhs. You could say, "Good luck!" Of the individual, but let's first take a look at the surroundings.

The public has a lot of trust in SBI because it is the largest public sector bank in India. Thus, they invested there. So what do shrewd investors do? They are aware that a bank's goals include making money, taking in public deposits, and lending money to other people. Where does the bank issue loans? They will generate income by making higher-interest loans to businesses. They conduct the essential research prior to lending their money, making a profit. Therefore, there is no assurance that purchasing bank shares will yield greater returns than purchasing a fixed deposit. Compound interest has a magical impact over a lengthy period of time.

Now let's go one step further. An investor who made a Rs. 50,000 investment in Infosys shares will receive Rs. 500 lakhs, or Rs. 1000 times that amount, after 20 years. The bank now charges a higher deposit rate when making loans to any kind of business. The corporation must be able to earn at least twice as much interest from borrowing money as it does from the bank.

For instance, if the bank charges an interest rate of 9.5 percent, the corporation must generate profits of at least 19 percent or greater. Instead, one could purchase company stock and gain from the promoters' dedicated efforts.

Similar to this, one father or grandpa only spent Rs 10,000 for 100 shares when Infosys went public in 1993. Divided and awarded bonuses, it eventually reached Rs155033600 in 2022. Without the right knowledge, investing could result in a loss of money. Don't enter the stock market and begin trading, then. Never perform it carelessly. A return of 15% to 18% is what you may anticipate if you make wise investments. Spend at least five years keeping an eye on the stock market.

Investing in Stocks: Common Sense

A major question is whether someone with a business background or any financial experts should invest in shares. Is it not just a cup of tea with no ulterior motives? For the record: Investors are not aware of the stock market. No matter their degree of experience, anybody is qualified. A person can invest in the stock market if they have a fundamental understanding of it.

In a survey conducted in the USA, two groups were created: one included 10-year-olds, and the other included Chartered accountants and analysts. It was mandated that each team select five shares and hold them for ten years.

The other set of ten-year-olds diligently researched promoters, competitors, financial analysts, and technical analysts while the first group made a selection of five shares. Additionally, they have chosen five shares.

After ten years, the 10 year olds in the first group have outperformed CPAs and financial specialists. What brought about that?

The children choose both the company's goods and the items they utilize. They have picked shares in companies like Barbie, Disney, and Cadbury. Children in Group 2 have only ever seen their products; they have never seen the real world.

Finding stocks using common sense

Consider the entire day, from the time you get up to the time you go to bed at night. Let's sit down and think about it. Take a close look at each item you use and the business that produced it or rendered the service. Let's practice jotting down the name of the business.

Business name - Usage

Because of the soap you use, you brush your teeth when you get up. Exactly how do you wash your hair?

Your favorite oil

The material you like is

What you are sporting

Your footwear is

The name of your gadget is

You make use of technology.

Riding a motorcycle

A car with four wheels

Your prescription drugs are produced using IT software.

You are allowed to list more than 50 daily items. You believe in the products as you utilize them. So why not invest in that company's stock? Is it true that if you buy shares, the promoter will work for you? What is required to make stock investments?

A person needs a bank account, a trading account, and a demat account in order to invest in stocks. Banks, full-service brokers, discount brokers, or both may be used to open an account for you. What is the bare minimum stock investment?

In the stock market, you can invest any amount of money; you can buy shares for as little as Rs. 1000. For instance, if Mr. Kulkarni, a 30-year-old investor, commits to investing $1,000 per month and increases his investment by 10% annually.

He would receive Rs 162 lakhs when he turns 60. Alternative investing options include mutual funds and systematic investing plans (SIPs). To support the time span in this case, consistency is required.

Being Aware Of The Stock Market's Hazards

The stock market drops and there is a recession. You won't perform effectively in the marketplace if you are unprepared and uncertain of what will occur. A few examples of investing opportunities include the bond market, fixed deposits, gold, government securities, real estate, and the stock market. Each tool has a certain amount of risk.

Even when the graph of the bond market or other fixed income instruments is continuously rising, the return is lower. It frequently falls below the inflation rate of decline. That implies that the value of money diminishes over time. There are frequent short-term ups and downs in the stock market. However, it has never had a negative impact on the Sensex of Nifty graph for three years running. If you want to make money on the market, you should invest for at least five years. When investing in the business, it's possible to lose money as well as get a bigger return.

- Numerous Risks
- Continuity Risk

It is a possible loss that could impact both the overall market and a specific market segment. It is a non-diversifiable risk that affects the whole asset class as well.

Systemic risks are beyond the control of investors, and they cannot be avoided. Many external causes, including the current geopolitical environment, governmental regulations, natural calamities, etc., frequently cause this. Covid's pervasive influence makes it a systematic risk.

Here are some classified Risks

- Political risk capacity for payment Inflation or Risk
- Foreign exchange risk
- Variations in interest rates due to natural disasters
- A country has a fiscal deficit if its expenses are larger than its income.
- Government policies
- Slow down in a recession.

Due to the fact that no investor or corporation has any control over any of these components, they cannot be diversified. You cannot escape this danger if you are investing in India or any other nation. it is, on a macroeconomic level.

Unknown Dangers

Unsystematic risks, which have a number of internal sources, only have an impact on the specific company or organization and do not have an impact on the market as a whole. Legislative changes, labor unrest in certain locations, and power or raw material shortages are examples of non-systematic causes. They go by the name of diversifiable risk.

Unsystematic dangers include things like large levels of business debt, new competitors entering the market, major staff turnover, significant operating costs, and negative cash flow, to name just a few.

Owning shares in a variety of companies helps disperse unsystematic risk. When investing in equities, one should diversify their portfolio over at least five industries. Many other industries, including the financial sector, are open to assistance.

- Areas of telecom and IT
- Pharmaceutical
- FMCG
- Metals
- Petrochemicals

For instance, because crude oil is a company's primary raw material, a decline in crude oil prices results in a loss for Reliance and a profit for Bharat Petroleum. Similar to the last example, if the value of the rupee falls, exporters make money while importers lose money.

The firm that creates the steel will lose money if the price of steel drops, whereas the person who purchases the steel, the company's raw material, will profit. You must diversify your stock holdings to reduce risk. As was previously said, invest in at least five distinct industries.

Purchase index funds. To invest in mutual funds, use a systematic monthly investment plan (SIP). Avoid buying equities that have a high beta or are very volatile. Never ever borrow money to buy stocks.

Dos and Don'ts of Investing in the Stock Market

According to Warren Buffett, the stock market is a means of transferring money from the impatient to the patient.

On the stock market, you might easily get a return of 22–23% and, over the Book of three to four years, see your money double. Think of this as a highly profitable source of income. You also need to set aside some time to study for it. You should observe some dos and don'ts when investing. Following are a few stock market no-nos:

Before you invest, research. One must pursue education for a minimum of five years in order to become a doctor and earn a living from it, and for a minimum of four years in order to become an engineer. Similar to that, it takes 4-5 years of study to become a CA. Therefore, how do you think someone who hasn't studied it would hope to make a good living? Therefore, become educated and seek for education.

Implement the knowledge with a little bit of- Lean and execute; set a low budget at first and raise it as your income rises.

Specify your financial goals. There are three basic categories of goals: medium-term goals, where it is a good idea to invest in both debt and equity; short-term goals, where it is never a good idea to invest in stocks. Equity is the best investment option for long-term goals that last longer than five years.

Invest money in the stock market that you won't need for four to five years. Give yourself enough time to complete your inquiry because you must make a timely analysis. market trends and some significant business news. All of these aspects will increase your trust in the business while also enabling you to make wise judgments.

Long-term stock market investing can be done in a variety of ways. Scalping is commonly referred to as high-frequency trading or quick trading since scalpers frequently buy and sell stocks every 15 to 20 seconds.

The simultaneous buying and selling of stocks during market hours is referred to as intraday trading. Swing trading is the practice of purchasing stocks with the intention of swiftly recouping the expenditures. For five to seven days, they retain inventory.

Purchasing stocks and holding them for 21 to 90 days constitutes positional trading. Making long-term trades: By retaining the stocks for between three and nine months, investors can profit from this type of investment.

Investment that will last a long time: nine months to many years. Investors are those who pursue medium- and long-term goals. Therefore, investing for the long run will enable you to prosper.

The saying "Don't put all your eggs in one basket" also applies to investing. Your investments shouldn't be concentrated in just one industry or stock. You can diversify your stock portfolio by holding it across a variety of industries and shares.

Purchase 10 to 15 different stocks to build a stock portfolio after conducting adequate research and analysis. Keep an eye on your stock holdings. Watch your portfolio occasionally, but not all the time. Hold onto the equities that are performing well and sell the ones that are losing money. Never anticipate a fourfold increase in the value of your investment within a few months; instead, be patient in the stock market to generate significant returns.

When trading stocks, avoid making these blunders. At all costs, disregard the falling average: Never average a stock while it is losing value or without first completing adequate investigation to understand why it is losing value repeatedly. Calculate the averages during upward trends instead.

Avoid taking out a loan to finance your investment in the stock market because you will have to pay interest on the loan each month and it will take years to see a return.

Never take advice without first conducting your own investigation. It's risky to purchase shares purely based on recommendations. Spend the money you've worked so hard to earn wisely. Instead of investing all of your money in the stock market, diversify your portfolio in accordance with your goals. Never make choices based on your emotions because they might have unfavorable effects.

It Is Your Money Grow It Big

Your financial situation is under your control. It is your responsibility to safeguard and expand your financial resources. Don't blindly rely on anyone for the management and investing of your money. Before beginning, mentally get ready for the 11 Secrets. And by reading this chapter, you'll be able to proceed.

It is essential that you have a firm understanding of your financial goals.

Write on a piece of paper while completing the assignment below. You can become wealthy by applying what you learn, not by reading.

A) Know what your financial goals are

a) What are your short-term financial goals?

1. These goals could persist for a full year.
2. What is your anticipated yearly income?
3. What expenses do you expect to have during the coming year?
4. Do you want to take a family vacation or buy some gadgets?

b) What are your financial goals for the near and long term?

1. These goals might be set for a year, four, or five years.
2. Take into account all the factors, such as the schooling of your children and possible property purchases.

c) Do you have any long-term financial goals?

1. Retirement planning,
2. child marriage, and
3. child higher education, which are frequently longer than five years.

Prior to anything else, be sure of your financial objectives; they must be in writing and not just in your head. If any adjustments are required, make them. In a 1999 article in Fortune magazine, it was said that people who had written plans for managing their investments often had five times as much money saved for retirement. Planning your investments helps you stay focused on the proper path, even though it does not guarantee success.

B) Concentration provides direction

The annual salary of a woman who worked for an IT company was Rs. 4 lakhs, but she had credit card and bank debt totaling Rs. 15 lakhs. She was having financial issues. When she learns about her shopping habits, she realizes that she likes to purchase expensive clothing. When she goes shopping, she always buys two to three dresses. In addition to all of that, she also purchases shoes and sandals. She has over twenty pairs of sandals and over a hundred designer outfits in her closet. Most of them stayed within the box. She owns fifteen watches, prefers to buy new ones, and rarely wears the ones she already owns.

Another individual who practices homeopathy has a lot of debt. He purchases the most recent flat-screen TVs, PCs, tablets, and cellphones since he appreciates utilizing cutting-edge technology in his daily life. I was surprised to learn that he enjoys purchasing a variety of different equipment when I learned about his shopping habits. Additionally, he had four iPods, all of which were the most recent models available at the time, although he rarely used them.

When I found out through investigation that they both had a monthly membership to the desired magazine, I thought, "One cannot undervalue the power of focus."

Similar to this, if you want to raise your money, focus on investment and growth. You can read trustworthy books on money and finances. You can become a member of an investing group and participate in a range of investment-related workshops.

C) Never rely on advice; instead, hone your investing techniques.

A common error is to rely on others to manage one's finances in the assumption that they will do it skillfully and in the person's best interests. You give your money your complete focus more than anyone else in the world. The greatest person to manage your finances is you, by yourself. Managing Personal finance is not a difficult topic to study. If your financial future is vital to you, you may pay the price by mastering it. Knowledge was not innate; it was acquired. They have knowledge and are always learning.

The quality of the advice will vary depending on the level of knowledge of the counselor. A visit to a professional is a smart idea; you should do this and educate yourself. Knowing the subject well will prevent you from blindly adhering to every advice and direction. Verifying the information is simple.

It's possible that there will be a conflict of interest if experts advise you based on the products they sell. Experts frequently get affiliate commissions for the recommendations they make. A knowledgeable associate with an insurance or mutual fund broker is likely to advise you to get life insurance and mutual funds. Most likely, a real estate expert will advise you to purchase some real estate. Think about how a stockbroker's associate expert could ask you to buy stocks, etc. You can base your recommendation on how much money the person who came up with the idea will get. This is why you are the best person to take care of yourself.

As was said earlier, there are a variety of abilities needed for both earning money and investing money. Any additional water will drain out of a container if one is provided for holding water but it has a hole in the bottom. Earning will put water in your jar, and the appropriate investment won't let any out. You could compare earnings and investment using that way.

So focus on developing the skills that will help you for the rest of your life rather than relying on advice or suggestions.

D) Strategic thinking

There is no such thing as a "get rich quick" scheme. Gluttony and the yearning for fulfillment are the root causes of the desire for rapid money. A process can be used to accomplish any objective. There is no quick fix for that. You can quicken the process by minimizing the learning curve, which is doable with a mentor or coach. You must still make an effort and take action. Work precedes achievement only in the dictionary. If not, being wealthy needs more and smarter work.

Thinking in the short term means focusing on what will help me right away. It is the practice of instant gratification. One must be patient and give money working time in order to gain from it. It takes time for seeds to grow into fully developed plants, and then a tree. You will miss a lot if you try to eat the seed before it grows into a tree. Fruit trees produce fruit indefinitely. You need to keep your cool, remain stationary, and handle the seed with caution.

It would help if you could see the bigger picture in order to free yourself from short-term thinking. When you have a limited perspective, you are thinking too soon. So start making plans for the upcoming 5, 10, or 20 years. Your level of belief increases with the size of the picture you can see. It is a picture if you can make it out clearly. It would help you break the habit of instant gratification. The better, sweeter fruits can be enjoyed for a long time afterward.

Learning more quickly is the best way to advance more quickly. You advance more quickly the more you learn and do. The assistance of a mentor and coach will speed up the process. Shortening your learning curve and knowing what to avoid doing and mistakes to avoid making based on their expertise are two advantages of learning from an expert.

Instead of seeking instant gratification, think long-term, take the larger picture into account, consult experts, and take action.

E) Giving back to society

We owe society something because it has kindly given us so much. As you contribute, more of nature will return to you, perhaps not initially or even from the same source. Although it's necessary to give back to society, you shouldn't anticipate receiving anything in return. When you are in the giver mode, your view of money will shift, which will eventually help you flourish. As a result, you'll start to think more creatively.

The First Tip is to Stay With One Company For at Least Ten Years

Multiple criteria must be specified in order to aid in the selection of the best products. The National Stock Exchange and the Bombay Stock Exchange both provide thousands of scrips. A criterion-based filtering method is required because all stocks underperform.

Even though purchasing shares only amounts to 0.0001% of the entire market value of the business, it makes us owners of it.

Not every year is good since the economy goes through several cycles. Like life cycles, business has booms, busts, and recessions. if the business has been in business for these ten years, gone through all the stages. As a result, it makes sense to invest in this company.

However, if one is considering investing in a recently created business, they should exercise caution. The success of the company will be determined by its long-term viability. Many businesses don't even survive five years. However, if a company has been around for at least 11 years, you may trust it as an investment. During that time, it will be simple to observe the company's operations, heritage, and performance.

I brought this chart here using the intradingview.com website.

For its clients' digital transformation, Infosys Ltd. offers technology, outsourcing, consulting, and next-generation digital services. Through its crucial goods and platforms, the company additionally provides a number of services. McCamish, Panaya, Meridian, Helix, Equinox, Wingspan, Edgeverve, Stater, and other instances of Infosys Finacle are available. The graph shows Infosys, an established company. It is simple to monitor the share's performance. It has delivered an incredible return.

Dabur India is a key player in the fast-moving consumer goods (FMCG) sector for food and personal care items. With a portfolio of more than 250 ayurvedic goods, Dabur India Limited is the fourth-biggest FMCG company in India and the largest natural health care and ayurveda company in the world.

With the help of its retail and wholesale network, Bata India manufactures and sells shoes and accessories. In addition to operating 1,569 stores around the nation, including franchisee locations, it has 3.06 million square feet of retail space. Under a number of recognizable brands, Bata offers footwear in India to both lower and upper market sectors. Bata, Power, Marie Claire, Scholl, North Star, Naturaiser, Bata Comfit, Weinbrenner, Ambassador, Mocassino, and Hush Puppies are a few of the names that are included under the brand umbrella.

HDFC Bank Ltd. is the biggest private-sector bank in India. The Housing Development Finance Corporation Limited (HDFC) was initially granted permission by the Reserve Bank of India to create a bank in the private sector. Established in 1994 as HDFC Bank Limited, HDFC Bank is a publicly traded financial institution with its registered office in Mumbai, India.

Among the banking and financial services it provides are treasury operations, wholesale banking, foreign currency trading, retail banking, and retail banking. A subsidiary of HDFC LtdHDFC Bank held around 19% of the business as of September 30, 2020. If you want to make money on the stock market, look at the data from the last ten years.

Promoters Must Own At Least 51% Of The Company

The third condition to consider is making an investment in a company where the promoter owns at least 51% of the company. Why is there a majority here?

Prompter has goals and objectives for the future of the business. He devotes his entire effort to making it better. The promoter is the individual with understanding of the business and future expectations.

However, if the promoter is selling a smaller portion, the incentive to expand and improve the business is lost. He puts in more effort and motivates his coworkers if he has larger stakes in the business.

Before making an investment in a business, the investor must conduct due diligence. A larger promoter holding increases the likelihood of growth. If the promoter purchases the company's shares on the open market, that bodes well for the future of the business. In this instance, the promoter is seeking the most profit and is confident in the operation of the company. Consider a few situations.

The second-largest paint firm in the world and the fourth-largest in Asia is based at The Painter Berger of Berger Paints India. Paint is produced and distributed by Berger Paints. In the industrial sector, Berger works with a number of illustrious clients. Force Motors, Tata Hitachi, Crompton, Orient, Havells, Mahindra & Mahindra, Hero MotoCorp, Royal Enfield, Tata

Motors, Ashok Leyland, Mahindra & Mahindra, Mahindra & Mahindra, and Mahindra & Mahindra are among companies in this category. Over 50,000 dealers and merchants make up the company's distribution network in India, which includes 180 stock sites.

Kuldipsingh Dhingra serves as chair. 75% of the business is owned by the promoter. Because of the size of his holdings, the promoter has unwavering faith in the company. His goals and vision for the business are strong and clear.

The prior ten years' stock price CAGR was 28%. As a result, money doubles in 2.6 years. India Havells Havells India Limited is a well-known manufacturer of power distribution equipment and a prominent fast-moving electrical goods company.

Consumer and commercial circuit protection devices, cables and wires, motors, fans, modular switches, home appliances, electric water heaters, air conditioners, power capacitors, and luminaires for residential, commercial, and industrial applications are just a few of the products that Havells dominates the market for.

The five brands owned by the company—Havells, Crabtree, Lloyd, Standard, and REO—are present in a variety of product areas. Rai Gupta Promoters, the company's originator, hold 59.4% of it.

Over the previous ten years, the stock price CAGR was 26%. In 2.8 years, it doubled. SRF SRF Limited is a global chemical corporation with operations in India that produces industrial and specialized intermediates. Fluorochemicals, specialty chemicals, packaging films, technical textiles, and coated and laminated fabrics make up the company's product line.

In the domestic market, SRF dominates the refrigerant market. Methylene chloride, chloroform, and carbon tetrachloride, which are used by customers in the pharmaceutical and agrochemical industries, are its major goods on the chloromethane market.

It saw further growth in market share as a result of the new chemical "F 600a". Ashish Bharat Ram holds a 50.7% promoter ownership share and serves as chairman.

Due to the 49% CAGR in stock prices over the previous ten years, money doubles every 1.5 years. As a general rule, promoters should own at least 50% of the shares if you want to invest and make money without risk.

A Higher Top Line

Sales or revenue are shown on the top line of the trading and profit and loss statement. The next criteria is for the company's sales to increase by at least 15 to 20 percent annually.

Here, both income and unit sales must increase. Total sales, if any revenue exists. The following year, it should increase from its present Rs 1000 level to Rs 1200. There are two reasons for the rise in revenue.

Price per Unit Increasing rise in unit sales. For instance, if 100 ballpoint pens were sold for Rs. 10, the sales would total Rs. 1000. The following year, 100 ballpoint pens would cost Rs 12, or Rs 1200. It should increase in line with unit sales, which is the issue in this scenario.

For a total of Rs 144, 120 ballpoint pens were sold for Rs 12. In addition, there ought to be more units. If one lakh automobiles were sold in the previous year, it makes sense for unit sales to rise to 1.2 lakh in the current year.

There are two ways to make money:

1. Operating Revenue
2. Operating Revenue

Operational operations, such as those from its main source, can generate operating revenue. Increased operating revenue is required. Selling a property without joining a real estate firm results in a useless profit for the seller.

In this case, our goal is to increase operating income rather than non-operating revenue. For instance, Eicher Motor sells more cars while simultaneously generating more money from each one. The consistency of per-unit sales growth is one criterion.

The Eicher Group's listed firm in India, created in 1982, and a prominent player in the country's automotive industry as well as a top producer of middleweight bikes worldwide is Eicher Motors Limited.

The share price was approximately Rs 150 in 2012; it will be approximately Rs 3600 in 2022. In less than three years, its costs have grown at a 37% yearly growth rate. In general, the script, whose sales climb by at least 20% annually, won't let you down.

Expansion Of The Bottom Line

It's different this time is one of the four investment expressions that entails the biggest risk. Lord John Templeton. The financial statements' profit and loss account's bottom line is referred to as net profit. The lifeblood of any business is profit. One's governing concept is the maxim of getting money. The firm cannot survive if there is no profit involved. A business must therefore consistently turn a profit.

When analyzing a company's financials, one should consider whether the profit is increasing annually. Look at the expansion during the previous 8–10 years. Pick a business whose annual net profit growth is at least 20%.

Profit Is The Result Of Revenues Minus Costs

Ethylamines, methylamines, derivatives of specialty chemicals, and pharmaceutical excipients are among the areas of expertise of Balaji Amines Ltd. These top products have the ability to manufacture derivatives, which are downstream products for the pharmaceutical and pesticide sectors, in addition to meeting the needs of specific users.

It is India's top producer of aliphatic amines. Over the past ten years, its compounded profit growth has increased by 27% annually.

In terms of revenue, one of the top five Indian IT services providers is HCL Tech, a well-known international provider of IT services. After becoming public, HCL Tech entered the world market in 1999 and has since concentrated on transformational outsourcing. It provides a wide range of services, including BPO, engineering and R&D services, remote infrastructure management, and software-driven IT solutions.

The company offers a variety of service delivery alternatives in important industry verticals by utilizing its broad global offshore infrastructure and network of offices in 46 countries. It has layers. The average yearly profit growth over the past ten years has been 23%. In determining stock valuation, net profit is considered.

The development, production, and marketing of finished dosages of specialty pharmaceutical quality are Ajanta Pharma's main commercial endeavors. Over the past ten years, its compounded profit growth has increased by 25% each year.

Tools For Locating Different Filters

Four criteria have been applied thus far to find different stocks. Numerous filters are still not being applied, as we will see in the following chapter. However, many of you are considering practical ways to find the stocks and buy the filters.

You can use a variety of techniques to locate the criteria and discover value stocks. I'll recommend the free gadget I use. Additionally, it will help you choose value stocks.

I'm using https://www.screener.in as my tool.

One of the best free resources for investigating a firm is this one.

On the website, first create a username and password.

Now go to the screens on the top middle and click.

Now go to create a new screen, and you can add the filters as much as you like.

I'll give you a few samples that you can copy and paste. However, do your homework. Price to Earning Industry PE, Average Return on Equity Ten Years > 15 Years, Return on Capital Employed Twenty Years, Market Capitalization One Thousand Years, Market Capitalization Thirty Thousand Years, Promoter Holding > Fifty Years, Debt to Equity Thirty Years, Sales Growth Ten Years > Ten Years, and Profit Growth Ten Years > Ten Years The average return on equity is over 20.

ten-year return > 20% Over Three Years, Over 20%, and Over Five Years Over 50 Free Cash Flow A higher percentage 20. Here are a few stocks that have shown value growth during the past 12 months, 3 years, and 10 years.

The return is higher than 20% over periods of ten years, three years, and one year. The company in the following scenario is debt-free. Example: Good Large Cap Companies AND Profit Growth 10 Years > 10 AND Market Capitalization > 5000 Return on Capital Employed during the past 10 years AND over 20 on average

As an illustration, consider the following formulas: 100*((High price - Current price)/High price)/10 AND 100*((Current price / Low price -1)) > 100 AND Current price > 10 AND Volume > 100000.

Leadership in Company

Every business requires capable leadership. A leader is someone who manages the expansion of the business. All of the leader's qualities—intelligence, capability, integrity, honesty, and vision—should be taken into account.

A strong leader can improve the organization's success despite its low overall performance. Let's examine more closely the leadership-related concerns we need to be aware of and research before making an investment.

Determine whether the market leader has a competitive edge in areas like distribution system, product quality, uniqueness of the product or services, unique technology, consistent capital base, etc. The company's goals and mission What are the prospects for the business and what are the management's growth expectations? What are their goals for the company, and what are their plans?

How long has the person in charge been working for the organization? Top executive positions ought to change often. The CEO and MD should not be changed frequently.

Background of the leader Finding out if that person is a party to a civil or criminal case can be done easily online. Any recent occurrences that raise questions about the subject's sincerity? Discovering the identity of the company's auditor is crucial. Background and standing in the industry of the auditor.

Additionally, there are a number of factors you shouldn't ignore. the compensation and salary of senior management staff. Do they receive a high salary, bonuses, or other forms of compensation? If true, this has an impact on the business. Then there are transactions between linked parties, in which one presents fictitious invoices and receipts, funds are moved to their accounts, and later management withdraws funds from those accounts.

Many outstanding leaders who never waver in their dedication, clarity, and honesty aid in the astounding success of their organizations. The chairman of the Tata Group was Ratanji Tata. Everyone respects him and has great faith in him since he upholds the principles of each Tata organization.

Tata Group companies include Tata Consultancy Services. It has provided IT services, consulting, and business solutions for more than 50 years, working with the most successful companies in the world as they undergo transition.

TCS offers a comprehensive range of integrated business, engineering, and technology services and solutions that are led by consulting and powered by cognitive technology. The graph emphasizes the advantages of investing in TCS for shareholders.

Reliance Industries Limited's chairman and managing director is Mukesh Ambani. The organization has advanced thanks to his talents, vision, and leadership.

In India's private sector, Reliance Industries Limited (RIL) is the largest Fortune 500 company. transforming from a producer of textiles and polyester to a participant with a varied portfolio in the energy, materials, entertainment, retail, and digital services industries. Nearly all Indians are impacted daily on an economic and social level by the array of goods and services offered by Reliance.

Wipro's founder and chairman was Azim Premji. He is a well-known philanthropist in Asia and is regarded as the Cazar of the IT Sector.

Wipro Ltd. is a multinational organization that provides consulting, IT, and business process services (BPS). The price skyrocketed from Rs. 138 in January 2012 to Rs. 700 in January 2022. Effective corporate management will increase shareholder wealth.

Any company on the screener can be selected to discover more details about it. Annual reports can be found if you enter and scroll down.

The most current alerts, rating updates, and scam calls will be sent to you. All of this information is beneficial when picking a company. Please try to get a general understanding without going into too much detail.

Debt-Free Company

Instead of turning to your buddies who only bet on football for advice, consult the wealthy who continue to gamble. Interest on a loan is an expense. Businesses that don't have debt will generate more revenue for you because they won't be paying interest. Because it has no loans, the firm is not required to pay interest to banks or other financial institutions.

Significant debt causes businesses to lose money, and investors experience poor returns. Visit screener.in to learn more about businesses without debt.

Enter Debt = 0 in the Create screen.

Then submit an application, and you'll discover a number of debt-free companies.

Compared to their equity, companies have comparatively few loans. There are businesses with debt-to-equity ratios that are considerably lower. Enter Debt to Equity is less than 0.30 on the create screen.

The website contains the annual report and the financials. Current Liabilities, Short-Term Borrowings, and Long-Term Borrowings are all included in this section of the company's financials.

You can learn more about the company's borrowings from that. Many loan defaulter enterprises have shut down due to high levels of debt. These businesses have defaulted on loans totaling over 10,000 crores.

Okay, business. Energy Monnet Ltd., Bhushan Steel Limited Inc., Amtek Auto Inc., Essar Steel Lanco Infrastructure Ltd., and Ispat. Here are a few businesses that are debt-free.

Laboratory Section

Divis Laboratories Ltd. primarily focuses on exports while producing intermediates, nutraceutical components, and active pharmaceutical ingredients (APIs). With 14,000 employees and a presence on the market in 95 countries, it ranks among the top pharmaceutical businesses in the world.

The price in April 2012 was Rs 398.

The price increased to Rs 4500 in April 2022.

at a rate of 27%, ten times or more. Sectoral CAGR Tanfac Aditya Birla Group and Tamil Nadu Industrial Development Corporation (TIDCO), which owns a 25% share in the company, collaborated to establish Tanfac Industries Ltd. in 1972. The business has been one of the biggest producers of hydrofluoric acid and its derivatives ever since it started carrying out commercial production in 1985.

It was Rs 16 in April 2012.

April 2022 saw a Rs 589 price increase.

There is a CAGR of around 43%.

Generally speaking, you should never put money into a company that has a lot of debt.

Net Operating Cash Flow Is Favorable

A company's cash flow is crucial to how well it runs. After the sale of its goods or services, the company should receive the cash flow immediately. One can only determine whether a corporation is producing cash flow by looking at its sales. What if the company appears to be doing well in terms of sales and net profit, but the sales aren't translating into revenue?

Thus, cash flow is crucial to any business. Three methods exist for earning money. From its main industry sectors

The cash that a company brings in through its main operations is known as operating cash flow. If an organization's main business is manufacturing, the money it makes from selling the products is its operating cash flow.

Loaning Money

Borrowing money results in a rise in cash flow. This cash flow, however, is unrelated to the company's routine business operations. As a result, it is not considered operating cash flow.

Sales Of Real Estate

Let's say the business sells its property or facility to raise the money. Because it is not a traditional business, operating cash flow is not taken into account. There are several ratios that can be used to evaluate the firm's financial health in terms of cash flow from operations.

OCF = Cash flow from core operations/Current Liabilities is the formula for calculating the operating cash flow ratio. The cash flow from operations is shown here as:

- Operations revenue minus non-cash-oriented costs minus non-cash-oriented revenues

- Debts to creditors, short-term loans, accrued expenses, etc. are all examples of current liabilities.

- A greater ratio is desired since it demonstrates how often net operating cash flow can be used to lower a company's liabilities.

- A ratio of one or above is excellent, whereas one or lower shows how financially precarious the organization is.

- Other ratios are calculated using cash flow, including net profit and sales with operational cash flow.

Before making an investment in any company, it is crucial to consider the following three factors:

- Sales growth: Also known as the top line - Annual growth must be at least 20%.

- The term "net profit" refers to growth that is at least 20% every year.

- It must be positive and at least 75% bigger than net income to qualify as net operating cash flow.

India Nestle

The international Swiss corporation Nestle has a division called Nestle India Limited. The business is involved in the food industry. In most product categories, it enjoys a dominant market position. The business is a pioneer in the food industry and sells a variety of products under the Maggi name. In the majority of product categories, such as beverages, prepared foods and culinary tools, chocolate and confectionery, milk products, and nutrition, the company is one of the top two competitors.

It cost $4200 in December 2011 and will cost Rs. 19800 in December 2021.

In 2011, it generated a net operating cash flow of Rs. 1158 crore.

In 2021, it will have a net operating cash flow of 2271 crore. Cash flow always triumphs because money is king.

Limited by Hindustan Unilever

The FMCG sector's Home Care, Beauty & Personal Care, and Foods & Refreshment segments are where Hindustan Unilever largely conducts business. The company sells primarily in India and has manufacturing plants all around the nation.

The graph is self-explanatory.

In March 2011, operating cash flow totaled 1924 crores.

In March 2022, the total was 9048 crores.

Return on Equity

A measure of a company's profitability in proportion to equity is called return on equity. The total of all assets minus all liabilities equals shareholder equity. Using shareholder equity, it calculates its profit. It determines how effectively the business turns equity into profits.

In other words, ROE assesses how effectively a business generates a profit for its shareholders. The worth of a corporation is its assets, which represent everything it owns, liabilities, which represent what it owes to other parties, and equity, which represents the residual value to shareholders. The balance sheet is made up of these three elements. Take a step back at this time.

The formula for calculating net profit is (Net Profit / Shareholder's Fund) * 100. Total equity is shareholder equity as well as reserves and surplus.

- The Profit and Loss Statement contains Net Profit.

- The balance sheet's equity.

- Any stock you want to buy must have a return on equity of greater than 15%.

One of the top international suppliers of design and technological services to a variety of areas, such as the automotive, media, communications, and healthcare industries is Tata Elxsi. Tata Elxsi has a global network of design studios, global development centers, and offices in addition to offering comprehensive services ranging from research and strategy through electrical and mechanical design, software development, validation, and deployment. Tata Elexi's return on equity is 37.2%.

The price increased from Rs 726 in April 2017 to Rs 8868 in April 2022. 65% is the usual return. See Abbott India right now.

One of the top international pharmaceutical corporations in India, Abbott India Ltd., sells the majority of its goods through local independent distributors. In 1944, it made its debut. ABOUT THE COMPANY Abbott Laboratories is the owner. The company has been in operation for more than 130 years and is present in more than 160 nations. It offers over 125 products in over a dozen therapeutic categories, including gastrointestinal, nervous system, and women's health. Additional topics include consumer health, multi-specialty (pain management, sleep issues, vitamin and nutritional supplements), and metabolic. In FY22, the company introduced ten new products across various therapeutic categories.

Abbott India's return on equity is 29.5%. In April 2017, it was Rs 4579. Additionally, the cost rose to Rs 17713/- in April 2022. It has produced average returns of 31% during the past five years. So let's look at one more instance.

Specialized organic intermediates and monomers are produced by Vinati Organics. It is the biggest producer of IBB and IBTS in the world. Since its founding in 1989, they have transformed from being a manufacturer of a single product to a fully integrated company that provides a variety of products to some of the biggest industrial and chemical firms in the US, Europe, and Asia.

- Its price was Rs 382 in April of previous year.
- In April 2022, prices increased by Rs 2100.
- Each year, the return is on average 41%.
- Furthermore, its ROE is 20.6%.

Return on Equity, which should be at least 15%, should never be disregarded if you want to succeed in the stock market.

Capital Employed Return

Shareholder contributions and loans are both considered forms of capital. Loans and shareholder monies make up the capital.

Consider a business that is earning Rs. 20,000 from each of its Rs. 50,000 loans and Rs. 50,000 shareholder funds. The calculated return on capital is (20000/ (50000 + 50000))* 100, or 20%.

Therefore, a business should generate at least 20% of its capital. Investing in a firm that can't make at least 20% is not a smart move. Let's use an illustration.

Plumbing and drainage systems are manufactured in the nation by Astral Poly Technik Ltd. Producing pipes and fittings for sewage, plumbing, agricultural, industrial, and fire sprinkler systems is the company's major line of business. In addition, it manufactures pipes for ducting, auxiliary goods, and urban infrastructure. Over time, it has also evolved into a firm dealing in adhesives.

- It cost Rs. 341 as of April 2017.
- It cost Rs. 2140 as of April 2022.
- Its average annual return over a five-year period was 44%.
- Its return on investment is 22.6%.

Think about one more example.

Jubilant Foodworks

Jubilant FoodWorks Limited is part of the Jubilant Bhartia Group, a large provider of food services in India. Its master franchise rights are a representation of Dunkin' Donuts and Domino's Pizza, two worldwide trademarks that serve various gastronomic market segments. The business also introduced Hong's Kitchen, the first locally produced brand, to the Chinese food industry. In India, the firm has the sole authority to set up and run Domino's Pizza locations. It is the biggest Domino's franchisee outside of the US. They are the sole Domino name bearers in Sri Lanka, Bangladesh, and Nepal.

In April 2022, the price rose from Rs. 101 to Rs. 591. Normal returns after five years are 42%. It has a 21.1% return on capital employed.

Never miss noticing Return on Investment of no less than 20% Let's take one more as an illustration.

Britannia Industries

Britannia Industries, one of India's largest food firms, has been in business for 100 years and generates more than Rs. 9000 Cr. in annual revenue. Britannia, one of the most dependable food producers, produces well-known brands in India, including Milk Bikis, Marie Gold, Good Day, Tiger, and NutriChoice.

The Britannia serves a range of delicacies, such as rusks, cakes, biscuits, bread, and dairy items like cheese, beverages, milk, and yogurt. In India's biscuit market, where it dominates, Britannia is one of the key competitors. The business offers a large selection of biscuits under several categories, such as glucose, Marie, cookies, crackers, cream, milk, and health.

Thanks to the company's PAN India network, its products are accessible to more than 50% of Indian homes and are sold in more than 50 lakh retail outlets across the country. It has a 41.5% return on capital employed.

Low-Cost Purchases

The PE ratio can be used to determine whether the market is overvalued or undervalued, or whether the company is correctly valued. PE is available to both general consumers and certain companies like Reliance, Infosys, TCS, etc.

Let's take a close look at the PE of the market. The Nifty and the Sensex are used as barometers or indicators in India. The PE determines when to enter the market at the best time.

One can tell if the market is operating effectively by looking at Nifty. Our country's top 50 businesses are referred to as the "Nifty 50." It is a thorough ranking of the top 50 Indian companies. For Nifty, there is a price-earnings ratio.

The price-earnings ratio, or P/E, tells me how much money I should invest and what kind of return I should anticipate. Based on this ratio, you can decide whether to invest in the market or not. Or when ought I to go into the market?

Before calculating the PE of a given firm, one should first calculate the PE of the entire market. The ratio has continually varied between 10 and 40 since the inception of the Nifty. It never does, but that doesn't mean it can't go below ten or above forty.

When the Nifty's PE is between 10 and 15, that is the ideal time to invest. You'll make a lot of money here. If the PE of Nifty is between 25 and 40, one shouldn't invest and, if at all possible, should get out of the investment.

The COVID outbreak was remarkable since it affected every country at once. Let's simplify things even more by calculating the price-to-earnings ratio. If the Nifty's PE is 10, investing Rs. 10 will yield a profit of Rs.

In this case, 10% would be the profit. If the Nifty's PE is 30, one must invest Rs. 30 to make a profit of Rs. Profits would be 3.33 percent. If the earnings are just between 3.33% and 6%, investing in fixed deposits or debt funds is advised.

How do you locate Nifty's PE?

Click the link I've supplied to go to the NSE website.

https://www1.nseindia.com/products/content/equities/indices/historical_pepb.htm

Select the time frame, which can be up to 365 days, and download it as an excel file. It will take you 10 to 15 minutes to download the last 15 to 20 years one at a time and enter them into an excel spreadsheet. It will help you decide when to enter or leave the market.

Let's now study specific businesses. We must determine the suitable stock price before investing in the stock market. It is crucial to understand whether the stock is now overvalued or undervalued.

I'll use an illustration. Consider if you had an option between these two attributes:You spend 25 lakhs to buy a house, and you may earn 10 lakhs each month in rent. However, you may purchase the identical home for 30 lakhs and rent it out for 15 lakhs per month. Which one of the two would you pick, then?

In terms of price, I plan to invest Rs. 30 lakh on a home. since my rent has increased by 50% as a result of a single 5 lakh rupee rise. It is clear that in this circumstance, I am getting more value for my money.

The stock market operates under the same principle. Before making a purchase, a person should consider the value of their money. What financial return are we getting on our investment?

Should you make outright purchases of both high PE and low PE stocks? Should you buy a stock at face value, for instance, if its PE is low? No, you shouldn't, and we'll talk about more things to be cautious of.

Let's start by understanding the PE ratio's calculation. The market value of the stock is shown as price per share. By dividing the share price by the earnings per share, the PE ratio is calculated. Earnings per share are calculated using the total number of shares, the net profit divided by the number of common shares, and the sum of the company's total earnings.

Say a stock is trading at $150 right now. Assume that the value of each share is $10. The PE ratio will be 15 if you split 150 by 10. What does this 15 mean right now? In other words, for every Rs. 15 you invest, you get back Rs. 15. However, it's unclear whether the number 15 is higher or lower. We can only comprehend this by way of comparison. What do we currently have as a point of comparison? Peer comparison is essential. Always evaluate it in relation to its competitors. You can contrast it with another company in the same industry to see whether 15 is less or more.

It is impossible to compare the PE of the FMCG company's stock to that of the IT stock. The industry should be the same for comparison. If the PE is lower, you ought to purchase the stock. Why do certain things affect PE levels?

Causes Of Huge PE

The cost of stocks is too high. It has a bright future and is a company that is growing quickly. What causes a stock with a low valuation and slow, negative growth to have a low PE? The future doesn't seem promising.

Only stocks with lower PE are significant. As a result, it is not advisable to choose shares with lower PE at random without considering other factors. What further elements have we noted as nine secrets to take into account? The optimum moment to invest is when a company's shares are cheap.

Since the stock PE is lower than the industrial PE in this case, the value is lower. So, where can investors locate stocks with PE values below industrial PE? Please feel free to utilize the screener.in

When you run a search utilizing Price to Earning Industry PE, all the companies are less expensive than Industrial PE. However, you shouldn't rely only on these factors; other factors, like sales, ROE, ROCE, profit, and a strong operating cash flow, are also crucial. Pick the business that is growing profitably, has a lower PE, and is getting operational cash inflows.

Follow The Trend

Even though we have studied a wide range of stock-related topics, it is important to comprehend the general direction of the stock market. We must first consider the market as a whole in order to determine the direction of the particular share. Choosing whether to buy through the PE of Nifty requires selecting a sector that is uptrending or whose future looks really bright. Therefore, determining the company's trend is the most important step.

When should I make stock investments? It's time to buy the stock after going through a number of fundamental analyses and costs. Is now the ideal moment to purchase that stock?

We must follow the stock's company's trend in order to locate the answer. Investors make the error of buying the stock each autumn and averaging the price. Such a grave error should never be made. A substantial number of investors bought YES Bank stock each autumn.

The stock's price began to decline around 270 and kept declining. People who attempted to average at every fall suffered large losses as a result. Be sure to first determine what led to the unexpected fall.

Similar to DHFL, investors tried to buy whenever the value dropped, but they were never successful. Never attempt to catch a falling knife.

Let's now continue on our journey. Technical analysis or the company's trend must still be taken into account even after the 10 elements described above have been taken into account.

With the use of technical analysis, you may examine the price range and trend. The market has been around for a while, so it is simple to follow a company's operations and price changes. Technical tools like charts can be used to do technical analysis.

To forecast future movements, one must concentrate on the graph of previous behavior. Let's choose something immediately. Although there are many technical tools available, I suggest going to https://in.tradingview.com and https://in.tradingview.com/chart/

The name of the company you wish to view must be entered. There are many different types of charts, including line, bar, and candle charts. The best option is a candle, so always go with that.

Decide on the time period right now. There are many different time periods, such as 15, 5, 1, 1, 1, an hour, a week, a month, etc. The chart will keep changing based on the era you choose.

Three major trends can be seen.

- Uptrend
- Downtrend consolidation or a lateral motion

But keep in mind that the stock market is always in a state of upheaval and never moves straight. Only in this way does it alter things. A stock's upward movement during an uptrend indicates fresh price increases.

Stocks typically fall during a downtrend, which denotes recent price lows. The stock fluctuates up and down within a predefined range during consolidation. Buy the stock if it is rising; avoid it if it is declining.

Since we are discussing long-term investment, you should scan the weekly and monthly charts for higher highs and lower lows.

Among the several technical analysis indicators, the RSI (Relative Strength Index) indicator is my personal favorite. The RSI's range is 0 to 100. The lower and upper bounds are, respectively, 0 and 100.

- The market is bearish and you shouldn't buy the stock if the RSI is below 40.

- It is also not advised to buy if the RSI is medium or sideways and between 40 and 60.

- You can purchase this stock if the RSI is positive and more than 60.

- You may now view any stock, including TCS, Reliance, and others.

- If the daily chart's RSI is higher than 60, the short term outlook is favorable.

- The medium-term trend is bullish if the RSI of the weekly chart exceeds 60.

- The long-term trend is bullish if the monthly chart's RSI reading is higher than 60.
- The name of it is 14 Days RSI.

Reliance's graph from 2011 to 2016 shows an RSI that is below 60, indicating that there was no uptrend throughout that time.

There was almost no return if one had been purchased this year. It would be obvious when to enter if one used these tools at that time.

Use the knowledge you've gained so far in practice. Any chart can be viewed, including those for Maruti, TCS, Reliance, and ITC. View the weekly and monthly charts as well. Practice is the key to success. Your chances of profiting increase as your understanding and use of trend analysis advance.

Final Words

The stock market is a great place to put money to work and gradually increase your wealth. Clearly define your financial goals before making an investment. You can succeed financially by placing long-term bets on carefully researched stocks. Think about the 11 principles you'll require before investing in cryptocurrencies.

The largest investors in the world are preparing to donate these Principals. These ideas apply to valuations, technical analysis, and fundamental analysis. You will only receive shares of the highest caliber when all of these filters are incorporated. Conduct thorough research before deciding how, when, where, and in which company to invest your money. And you'll already be ahead of many private investors if you give your financial future planning at least as much thought as you would devote to buying a new car. You might potentially earn a lot of money with a little effort, but first you must conduct your research.

The stock market relies heavily on risk management. Systematic and unsystematic risk are the two categories of risk, as was previously mentioned. The risk of a loss is significantly reduced by using these 11 filters, and the gain is exponential. Although it is impossible to predict the market, it is always a good idea to use a seatbelt while driving.

Bear markets, recessions, and depressions cannot be avoided, but by spreading your equity holdings among four to five industries and 14 to 15 shares, you can reduce your risk. Buy lucrative stocks and cut your losses. I also put some of my money into reputable stocks because they offer great returns on long-term investments, which I can leverage to my advantage. I advise making long-term use of the filters and help if you want to increase your fortune.

Don't miss out!

Visit the website below and you can sign up to receive emails whenever Book Wave Publications publishes a new book. There's no charge and no obligation.

https://books2read.com/r/B-A-LAFAB-SGKNC

Connecting independent readers to independent writers.

Also by Book Wave Publications

How To Make Money In Stocks Value Investing Strategies

www.ingramcontent.com/pod-product-compliance
Lightning Source LLC
LaVergne TN
LVHW022026200926
848481LV00007B/2565
9798223392743